Guide to Rocks and Minerals

Marble
and Other Metamorphic Rocks

Chris and Helen Pellant

GARETH**STEVENS**
GS
PUBLISHING
A Member of the WRC Media Family of Companies

Please visit our Web site at: www.garethstevens.com
For a free color catalog describing Gareth Stevens Publishing's list of high-quality
books and multimedia programs, call 1-800-542-2595 (USA) or 1-800-387-3178 (Canada).
Gareth Stevens Publishing's fax: (414) 332-3567.

Library of Congress Cataloging-in-Publication Data

Pellant, Chris.
    Marble and other metamorphic rocks / Chris and Helen Pellant.
       — North American ed.
          p. cm. — (Guide to rocks and minerals)
       Includes bibliographical references and index.
       ISBN-13: 978-0-8368-7907-0 (lib. bdg.)
    1. Rocks, Metamorphic—Juvenile literature. I. Pellant, Helen. II. Title.
    QE475.P445   2007
    552'.4—dc22   2006036239

This North American edition first published in 2007 by
Gareth Stevens Publishing
A Member of the WRC Media Family of Companies
330 West Olive Street, Suite 100
Milwaukee, WI 53212 USA

This U.S. edition copyright © 2007 by Gareth Stevens, Inc.
Original edition copyright © 2005 by Miles Kelly Publishing.
First published in 2005 by Miles Kelly Publishing Ltd., Bardfield Centre
Great Bardfield, Essex, U.K., CM7 4SL

Gareth Stevens editorial direction: Mark J. Sachner
Gareth Stevens editor: Alan Wachtel
Gareth Stevens art direction: Tammy West
Gareth Stevens designer: Scott M. Krall
Gareth Stevens production: Jessica Yanke

Picture credits: All artwork courtesy of Miles Kelly Artwork Bank. Photographs from the Miles Kelly Archives:
Castrol, CMCD, CORBIS, Corel, DigitalSTOCK, digitalvision, Flat Earth, Hemera, ILN, John Foxx, PhotoAlto,
PhotoDisc, PhotoEssentials, PhotoPro, Stockbyte p. 11, p. 21, p. 27; Cover and title page © Diane Laska-Swanke;
All other photographs courtesy of Chris and Hellen Pellant.

Printed in Canada

1 2 3 4 5 6 7 8 9 10 10 09 08 07 06

COVER: A piece of marble.

Table of Contents

Words that appear in the glossary are printed in
boldface type the first time they appear in the text.

What Are Rocks and Minerals?

- Many types of rocks and minerals exist on Earth. People use them in many ways. Rocks and minerals are also beautiful to look at.

- Minerals are solid natural substances that are made of the same material all the way through. Rocks are made of minerals. They are solid, but rocks are not the same all the way through.

- One example of a mineral is quartz. If you look at a **crystal** of quartz, you'll see that it is made of the same stuff all the way through. No matter how big the piece of quartz is, it is made of the same type of material all the way through.

- Granite is a type of rock. If you look at a piece of granite, you can see that it is made of different types of minerals. Quartz, mica, and feldspar are among the minerals in granite. Limestone and marble are two other types of rock. Both contain the mineral calcite.

- Scientists who study rocks and minerals are called **geologists**.

- Geologists place different types of rocks into groups. These groups are based on how the rocks form. **Igneous rocks** form from **molten** material that cooled deep within Earth or from molten material that erupted onto Earth's surface out of volcanoes. **Sedimentary rocks** form out of layers of tiny particles. **Metamorphic rocks** form when Earth's forces heat or squeeze rocks so much that they change into a different type of rock.

- Rocks began to form about 4 billion years ago — as soon as Earth began to cool.

- The first rocks were igneous rocks. Sedimentary rocks form from rocks that have broken down. Some of these rocks are heated and squeezed until they become metamorphic rocks. If rocks are buried deeply enough in Earth's crust, they melt.

ABOVE and BELOW: Minerals can have bright colors and fine crystal shapes. The yellowish mineral ettringite (*above*) forms in six-sided crystals. Gneiss (*below*) is one example of a type of metamorphic rock.

What Are Metamorphic Rocks?

- Metamorphic rocks are any rocks that have been changed by heat, pressure, or a combination of heat and pressure within Earth.

- The process by which these forces change rocks is called metamorphism. The changes that result from metamorphism are called metamorphic changes.

- Most metamorphic changes take place at temperatures between 392°Fahrenheit (200°Celsius) and 1,292°F (700°C).

- The pressure at which metamorphic changes take place is up to 6,000 times greater than Earth's **atmospheric pressure.** These changes can occur at a depth of more than 12 miles (20 kilometers).

  - In contact metamorphism, heat is the only force that changes rocks.

    - In regional metamorphism, both heat and pressure cause rock to change.

      - Although metamorphism uses heat, it does not involve melting rocks.

      - Metamorphism can change the **chemical** make-up and structure of rock.

LEFT: Garnet is a type of mineral that forms in many of metamorphic rocks, especially schist. It can be cut and **faceted**, and it is used as a semiprecious **gemstone.**

- Metamorphism often removes the layers in sedimentary rock.
- Metamorphism can be strong or weak. The stronger it is, the more it changes rocks and the harder it is to identify the original rock.
- The metamorphism that changes rock into slate is weak. For this reason, fossils are sometimes found in slate. Strong metamorphism destroys the fossils that some rocks contain.
- Some of the oldest rocks in Earth's crust are gneisses. Gneiss is created by very strong metamorphism.

RIGHT: Where rocks are highly folded, deep underground, they are altered by regional metamorphism. Rocks near magma are changed by contact metamorphism.

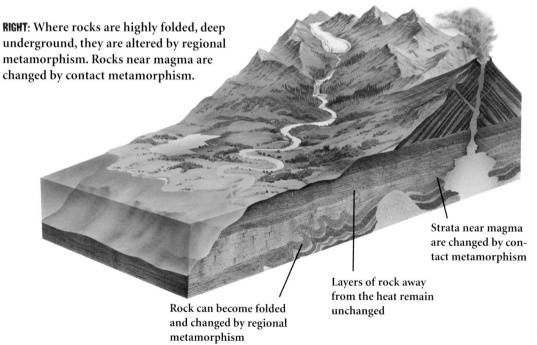

Strata near magma are changed by contact metamorphism

Layers of rock away from the heat remain unchanged

Rock can become folded and changed by regional metamorphism

Contact Metamorphism

- Contact metamorphism is the changing of rocks by heat from nearby **magma** or **lava**.

- The region around a mass of magma in which rocks have been changed is called a metamorphic aureole.

- A lava flow can only change the rocks that are below it.

- The amount of contact metamorphism depends on the size of the heat source and how close it is to the rock it heats.

- The metamorphic aureole around a large **batholith** may be a few miles wide.

- A small sill, dike, or lava flow may change rocks only a few inches away.

- Rocks right next to the heat source are changed greatly. Rocks far away from the heat source are changed less.

- Dark-colored spots and clusters of minerals are often found in shale that has been affected by contact metamorphism.

- When heated, the sedimentary rock limestone becomes the **crystalline** metamorphic rock marble.

- Contact metamorphism changes the sedimentary rock sandstone into a hard, crystalline metamorphic rock quartzite.

BELOW: The sloping rock surface on the right is made of granite. When it formed deep underground nearly 300 million years ago, intense heat from the magma out of which it is made changed the nearby sedimentary rock into the metamorphic rock hornfels. Hornfels is visible on the left of the picture.

Marble

- Marble is formed by the contact metamorphism of the sedimentary rock limestone.

- Heat from magma or lava causes the mineral calcite in limestone to **recrystallize**. After it recrystallizes, it is still calcite, but its crystals have a different form.

- As limestone recrystallizes, its layers and the fossils in it are destroyed.

- Pure limestone changes into a very light-colored marble with very few colored **veins**. Often, this type of marble has a sugary texture.

- Limestone that contains clay, other sedimentary material, or minerals changes into marble with colorful veining.

- The minerals brucite, olivine, or serpentine give marble a greenish color.

- For more than 2,500 years, people have used marble for art and decorations. It is good for these uses because it is easy to shape and polish.

- The ancient Greeks and Romans used marble to make statues.

ABOVE: This is an abandoned marble **quarry** on the Isle of Iona, in western Scotland. Much of the marble from this quarry was shipped to Europe. This quarry closed in 1914.

- When the sedimentary rock sandstone is changed by contact metamorphism, it turns into quartzite.

- Sandstone needs a large amount of heat to change it. Heat from magma, lava, or just from being buried deep within Earth causes the bits of quartz in sandstone to grow and join together or recrystallize.

- Quartzite is found very close to large batholiths because they give off the large amounts of heat needed to change sandstone.

- Sandstone's fossils are destroyed by the time it becomes quartzite.

- Slight traces of sandstone's layers may remain in quartzite.

LEFT: Originally sandstone, this quartzite is now a mosaic of quartz crystals. The original layers in the rock have disappeared.

- Sandstone has small spaces between its grains. Quartzite does not have these spaces. Because it does not have spaces, quartzite is heavier than sandstone.

- Quartzite is a light-colored rock with a sugary texture.

- Quartzite is made almost entirely of quartz. It may also contain small amounts of feldspar and other substances.

- Because it contains so much quartz, it is hard and it resists **weathering**.

- Quartzite is quarried and used in construction.

Cataclasis and Mylonite

- Faults are breaks in the rocks of Earth's crust where the rock surfaces move against one another. When rock surfaces move against each other in a fault, earthquakes occur.

- Fault breccia is a sedimentary rock made from small pieces of rock that is common in faults.

- Large-scale faulting crushes rocks and changes them through a type of metamorphism called cataclasis. In cataclasis, the grains in a rock are broken and rotated.

- Mylonite is a metamorphic rock that is made through cataclasis.

BELOW: The pale mineral seen in this close-up picture of mylonite is quartz.

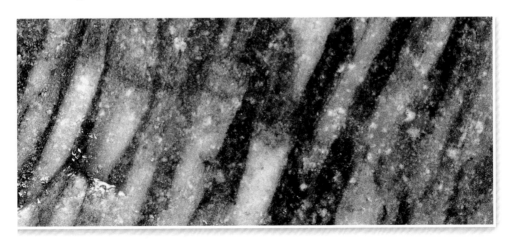

- After a lot of movement occurs over time in a fault, ground-up rock and any minerals that are in the fault are changed into mylonite.
- Mylonite breaks in thin plates.

BELOW: The Glencoul thrust fault, located in Sutherland, Scotland, is an area in which mylonite is found.

Regional Metamorphism

- Regional metamorphism affects rocks over large areas of Earth's crust.

- Regional metamorphism occurs when mountains are formed. Often this involves the moving of Earth's **plates.**

- Regional metamorphism changes rocks with both heat and pressure.

- The changes involved in this type of metamorphism may take tens of million of years.

- Some of the oldest rocks in Earth's crust have been affected by regional metamorphism. These rocks are about 3.5 billion years old.

- Mountain building pushes some rocks very deep into Earth's crust. The deeper a rock is pushed into Earth's crust, the more it is changed by regional metamorphism.

  - Rocks that have been changed a lot by metamorphism are called high-grade rocks.

  - Gneiss is the highest-grade rock. Schist is a lower-grade metamorphic rock. It is formed higher up in Earth's crust than gneiss.

LEFT: Gneiss

BELOW: Regional metamorphism occurs in the roots of mountain chains.
Deep below the Alps in Switzerland, slate, schist, and gneiss are forming.

Slate

- Slate forms at the edges of mountain regions. It is one of the lowest-grade metamorphic rocks.

- Slate started out as the sedimentary rocks mudstone.

- Slate is a dark-colored rock that is made of grains and crystals too small to be seen by the naked eye.

- Slate is known for the way it splits into neat, thin layers. Because it splits so easily, slate is used for roofing and gravestones.

- Some slate still contains fossils, but they are often squashed or stretched by the metamorphic forces.

- Some slate contains small crystals of pyrite, or fool's gold.

- Green slate gets its color from the mineral chlorite. Chlorite grows as result of metamorphic forces.

- Slate is found in many places. In the United States, it is found in California. In Britain, it is found in North Wales, Devon, and Cumbria, Scotland. Onijarvi, Finland, and Vosges, France, are also known for slate.

RIGHT: This thin, flat piece of slate contains crystals of fool's gold.

Schist

- Schist forms at higher temperatures and pressures than slate.
- The heat and pressure needed to make schist occur deeper within Earth's crust and closer to the center of mountain areas than that needed to make slate.
- Schist contains the minerals quartz, feldspar, and mica. Its silvery color comes from mica. The mica in schist may be light-colored muscovite or dark-colored biotite.
- Wavy bands run through schist because of the way its minerals have lined up during metamorphism.
- The minerals garnet, kyanite, hornblende, and epidote can form in schist during metamorphism.
- A lot of schist occurs in the European Alps. Rocks in this region were folded and changed by heat and pressure about 40 million years ago.

BELOW: Schist has wavy bands running through it. This piece also has reddish garnet crystals.

ABOVE: The hills and mountains of the Scottish Highlands are mostly made of schist.

Gneiss

- Gneiss — pronounced "nice" — is formed by the extreme heat and pressure deep in Earth's crust. The heat and pressure that turn rock into gneiss will change any type of rock that is exposed to it.

- Gneiss is the highest grade of metamorphic rock.

- Gneiss is made of alternating bands of different dark- and light-colored minerals.

- The light-colored bands in gneiss contain minerals such as quartz and feldspar. The darker bands in gneiss contain minerals such biotite, mica, and hornblende. The make-up of gneiss is similar to the make-up of granite.

- Some gneiss contains other minerals, such as quartz or garnet. Gneiss that contains patches of quartz that look like eyes is called augen gneiss. *Augen* is German for "eyes."

LEFT: The dark- and light-colored bands in gneiss are easy to see.

- Wherever it is found, gneiss is usually the oldest rock. Some gneisses are more than 3 billion years old.
- Some large areas of Earth's continents, such as the Canadian shield, are made mostly of gneiss. These areas have younger rocks on top of their gneiss.
- Gneiss is a hard and durable rock. It is used in the construction of roads.

ABOVE: This rugged landscape of low gray hills is made of gneiss.

Eclogite

- Eclogite forms under great heat and pressure in the deep roots of mountain chains.

- Geologists have discovered that eclogite is made from **basalt** lava that has melted and then recrystallized under great pressure.

- Eclogite is a dark-colored rock that is made of the minerals pyroxene and garnet. Its pyroxene is yellowish or green, and its garnet is red.

- Other minerals that occur in eclogite include rutile, pyrite, corundum, and kyanite.

- Eclogite contains large crystals that are easy to see with the naked eye.

- The minerals in eclogite may be arranged in alternating bands or they may be scattered through the rock randomly.

- Although eclogite is a rare rock, it can be found around the world. California, the European Alps, Japan, and South Africa all have eclogite.

RIGHT: Eclogite can be a very attractive rock, with masses of red garnet and green pyroxene. This piece of eclogite is from Norway.

FASCINATING FACT

Eclogite is important to geologists because they use it to learn about the deepest part of Earth's crust.

Calcite and Rhodochrosite

- Calcite is one of the most common minerals.

  - Marble, a metamorphic rock, is made of calcite. Calcite is also the main mineral in the sedimentary rock limestone. Limestone is the rock that heat and pressure change into marble.

    - Calcite defines point 3 on Mohs' hardness scale. Mohs' hardness scale is a ten-point scale for expressing the hardness of minerals. Each point on the scale is represented by a certain mineral.

      - Calcite forms in sharply pointed six-sided crystals or flattened six-sided crystals.

LEFT: Calcite crystals with flattened tops are called nail-head crystals.

- Rhodochrosite is a mineral with a rich, deep pinkish-red color. Its red color comes from the **element** manganese.

- Although rhodochrosite most commonly crystallizes in hydrothermal veins, it can also crystallize through contact metamorphism.

- Because of its attractive color, rhodochrosite is cut and polished to make ornaments.

Kyanite and Garnet

- Kyanite and garnet are two of the most attractive minerals that develop during metamorphism.
- Kyanite forms in rocks affected by the great heat and pressure of regional metamorphism.

- Schist and gneiss are the metamorphic rocks in which kyanite usually occurs.

- Kyanite is often various shades of blue, but it may also be pink, green, gray, or yellow.

- The hardness of kyanite varies between 4 and 7 on Mohs' hardness scale, depending on the direction in which it is scratched.

- There are many different types of garnet. "Garnet" is actually the name for a family of minerals.

LEFT: This mass of blue, blade-shaped kyanite crystals is from Brazil.

- Garnet crystals usually form in complex shapes with parallelogram-shaped faces.
- Garnets can be red, dark red-brown, green, or orange.
- Because garnet is harder than quartz and has attractive colors, it is used as a gemstone.

ABOVE: This is the red-brown variety of garnet called grossular.

Glossary

atmospheric pressure: the weight of the air surrounding Earth at sea level

basalt: a type of dark-colored, fine-grained igneous rock

batholith: a very large mass of igneous rock that was once magma

chemical: having to do with materials as studied by the science of chemistry

crystal: crystal: a piece of a transparent mineral that can have a shape with a regular arrangement of flat surfaces and angles or a rounded shape

crystalline: having to do with or like crystals

element: one of the simplest natural substances

faceted: cut in a shape with many small, flat surfaces

gemstone: a stone that is cut, polished, and used in jewelry

geologists: scientists who study the layers of Earth and the rocks and minerals that make up Earth's crust

igneous rocks: rocks that formed from the cooling and hardening of magma

lava: molten rock that flows from a volcano or the rock that forms when this substance cools

magma: molten material inside Earth that cools to become igneous rock

metamorphic rocks: rocks that have been formed by the forces of heat and pressure within Earth

molten: melted

ornaments: things added for decoration

plates: the large, moving sections of Earth's crust

quarry: a place where rock is dug out of an open pit

recrystallize: to change from one form of crystal to another

sedimentary rocks: rocks that formed from the small pieces of matter deposited by water, wind, or glaciers

veins: long, narrow deposits of minerals in rocks

weathering: the wearing down of rock by the effects of wind, rain, and changes in temperature

For More Information

Books

Experiments with Rocks and Minerals. True Books: Science Experiments (series). Salvatore Tocci (Children's Press)

Rock Cycles: Formation, Properties, and Erosion. Earth's Processes (series). Rebecca Harman (Heinemann)

Rocks and Minerals. Science Fair Projects (series). Kelly Milner Halls (Heinemann)

Rocks and Minerals. Science Files (series). Steve Parker (Gareth Stevens)

Rocks and Minerals. Discovery Channel School Science (series). Anna Prokos (Gareth Stevens)

Web Sites

The Dynamic Earth: Plate Tectonics and Volcanoes
www.mnh.si.edu/earth/text/4_0_0.html
From the Smithsonian Institution, this Web site features multimedia presentations on how Earth's plates move and how volcanoes work.

The Dynamic Earth: Rocks and Mining
www.mnh.si.edu/earth/text/3_0_0.html
Also from the Smithsonian Institution, this Web site features great pictures.

Rock Hounds
www.fi.edu/fellows/payton/rocks/index2.html
Information about how rocks are formed and how to collect rocks, along with quizzes and puzzles.

Publisher's note to educators and parents: Our editors have carefully reviewed these Web sites to ensure that they are suitable for children. Many Web sites change frequently, however, and we cannot guarantee that a site's future contents will continue to meet our high standards of quality and educational value. Be advised that children should be closely supervised whenever they access the Internet.

Index